Retirement

Back to Basics

Susan Kersley

RETIREMENT: BACK TO BASICS

First edition 2021.

Updated 2023

Table of Contents

Chapter 1 GET READY TO RETIRE

When asked about retirement, people say:

- *'I did not know before I retired how difficult I would find it organising my time.'*
- *'I've been too busy during my working life to look after myself. I guess I have to take the consequences now,'*
- *'I'd love to have some new and exciting things to do but I can't seem to motivate myself,'*
- *'I've spent such long hours at work for so long that I don't really know what to do with my day.'*
- *'I hate the thought of becoming a couch potato, just sitting around all day watching TV and eating, but I can see it might be easy to slip into that without realising what was happening'*
- *'I would like to have a life after work.'*

They've been told that retirement is about:

- *relaxing*
- *taking things easy*
- *exploring new hobbies*
- *travelling to places they wanted to visit*
- *improving relationships*
- *getting fitter*
- *growing older*

It's also about confidence, persistence and motivation.

Successful retirement is about planning. It means deciding what you want to do and how you want to spend your time and your money. It's about being open to opportunities and taking actions to achieve what you want, so you can have a fulfilling and interesting life after work.

Years ago, **life expectancy** was short so most of us wouldn't have lived beyond our 30s or 40s. Some would have succumbed to infection or other disease, and others died in childbirth.

We can expect to live for at least threescore years and ten or twenty. Many people are living into their nineties and hundreds. The generation of people retiring now are **younger in outlook and fitter in body** than their counterparts in the past (and maybe in the future too), and may live for many years with exciting times in their life after work.

A good metaphor is a rehearsal for a play, with learning the lines and actions, compared to going on stage without having seeing the script and expecting a faultless performance.

As you **prepare for retirement,** you will be like the well-rehearsed actor, ready to respond to the audience's reaction but with a path forward already planted in your mind.

Are you ready to learn the script, or do you want to move into the next phase of your life with no preparation? Are you going on this journey, not knowing where to, or what you want?

It's useful to have a plan, so however much you try to take a path this way or that, you can always come back where you were and move forward to your goal.

Getting ready for retirement is about **planning your itinerary for the next stage of your life,** enabling you to travel through the transition from work to retirement and encouraging you to explore the highways and byways as you go. It's an opportunity to move your way as you think about your retirement.

You can take a chance and walk onto the stage of life with no preparation, or you can make life much easier for yourself.

- *Are you apprehensive about retirement?*
- *How will you manage without the routine of work?*
- *Will you cope with your change of identity?*

This book provides you with simple strategies to enable you to get ready for retirement and have a wonderful life.

Although you may miss **the routine of work,** you have the opportunity, when you retire, to live and do things you haven't been able to do for years. You can access opportunities that leaving work offers.

You will discover who you are when you let go of your working identity and find how this life transition can excite and be fun. Here are some choices open to you:

- *Exploring new opportunities*
- *Discoverin abilities, you weren't aware of*
- *Satisfying long held dreams*
- *Spending time on your own*
- *Being in the company of others*
- *Get paid for what you do*
- *Becoming a volunteer*
- *Making music alone or with a group*
- *Becoming fit*
- *Swimming*
- *Joining a ramblers' group*
- *Going to a gym*
- *Reassessing your life*

Successful retirement needs:

- *an intense desire, or passion*
- *deciding to do something*
- *determination to do whatever is necessary*

- *a clear focus to achieve*
- *a sense of direction*

Imagine floating forward towards the end of your life and think about how you would feel if you don't make the changes you want. Then **visualise yourself** in your future, having done all the things you really want to achieve in your life. In order to achieve these, what do you have to do now?

There is something special about setting out on a personal journey, going through the difficulties of any personal change, and finally reaching the goal you set for yourself.

You will feel a sense of satisfaction when you achieve what you want, especially if you've not done it previously. It could be something as simple as tidying some clutter or clearing out old clothes, or as complicated as planning a journey around the world.

For example, if you are discovering how to use a new camera, you feel a sense of fulfilment when you have taken a set of photographs and viewed them on your computer. Even though you know you have a lot more to learn, you are pleased about the initial part of the process.

Change may take a moment or go on for a long time, but when you plan to do something over months or years, then finally reach your goal, there is a sense of outstanding achievement.

Overcoming objections is your next task. When you talk about the changes you want, or goals you hope to achieve, it is a common experience that some people will tell you it is impossible and you won't be able to do that. Yet, when you decide to do something, and continue despite objections, there is a wonderful sense of completion when you finally succeed.

There might be a valuable reward when you reach your goal, yet the actual value isn't necessarily vital. For example, a certificate to show you passed an exam is only a piece of paper, yet the value of that reward is tremendous and gives a great sense of personal achievement. Something that shows you and others what you've been through on your journey of change can enhance your own sense of its value.

If you believe things can't change unless someone else does something different, or if you hope that your life will change on its own, remember the power is **in your own hands**.

The best way to start the change you want is for **you** to do something that stimulates change in others.

Take action for things to be different. Just like a spreadsheet, when one thing changes, everything else alters too.

Retirement is a time to re-think your daily routine and find new and exciting opportunities of what to do when you no longer have to keep to the daily work routine.

"Those who think they have not time for bodily exercise will eventually have to find time for illness." Edward Stanley, Earl of Derby (1826-93)

These words are even truer today. If you spend a large part of your working day in front of a computer and your leisure time watching television, then your level of fitness may be inadequate. Perhaps you know this already. Have you joined a gym or playing a sport, but got fed up or too tired to continue after a few weeks?

Exercise must be an important part of your new daily or weekly routine. It doesn't have to be 'over the top.' It just needs to be something you can fit into your lifestyle, easily. Choose an exercise you enjoy and do regularly without due stress.

Walking is one of the easiest ways to achieve this. Do it every day by going out with no special equipment. Do it anywhere, on your own or with company. If you go by bus walk to the next bus-stop. Always take the stairs instead of a lift and don't begrudge any walking that is necessary during your day. If you can do this in the countryside, beside the sea or in a park, there are even more benefits from getting away from polluted air in towns and cities. Also consider yoga and swimming as other ways to help your health and well-being during your retirement.

Exercise is vital to do regularly because it will keep you well for longer, with your heart beating strongly, your joints more mobile and your body more flexible and be able to cope with whatever happens as you get older and if you become ill your chance of a speedy recovery increases.

Happiness during this time of your life is likely to be an overwhelming priority. How will you decide what to do and start taking some definite action towards what you want?

Too many people talk about 'one day I'll do this or that' and yet they never get around to doing any of it. If you want the fulfilment of a life well lived and you are clear about what you need to accomplish during the rest of your life, then make a commitment to start.

New habits take repeating at least twenty-one times for them to embed into your unconscious mind, so it takes little things repeated day-by-day to make a difference to your big picture. Pick something that differs from your normal routine. Changing any habit makes it easier to change others. If you find it difficult to start, try something apparently unconnected. For example, change what you eat for breakfast to the sort of clothes you wear and notice what happens.

There can be a **sense of serenity** when you go with the flow, and things will eventually move forward. It depends on you, on your preparatory work, on the steps you decide to take initially and, on your passion to enjoy a wonderful, exciting and rewarding retirement.

Chapter 2 SUPPORT

Are you worried about how to cope with retirement? Everyone, including you, can benefit from support.

Everyone needs support at different times in their life. It's important to find a person or group to support you at a time of transition. This may be someone not involved in your life, so you can talk openly and not feel judged by them. They should accept what you tell them without criticism. In that way, you can bounce ideas and discover what you need to do.

If you had to leave work because of ill health, or on suspicion of malpractice, then what's happening may upset and confuse you. You may be angry about how life treated you, or guilty about something you did, which became much bigger than you imagined it could. In these circumstances, it may seem impossible to appreciate life again.

It's important to enjoy life, have a laugh, see the funny side of those situations that upset or frustrate you. When someone gives you words of comfort and guidance, it's reassuring to know that others have been through similar experiences.

Decide what you want because then you can seek the right person to support you. You may want practical help with physical tasks or someone to talk to about your emotional or spiritual needs. You decide and ask for it. Don't say 'I want someone to help me,' without specifying what you want, because 'helping you' may be mis-interpreted.

When you are about to enter a new stage in your life, such as retirement, you worry about how you solve problems. Everyone, including you, needs and can benefit from support, especially at certain times in your life. These times of transition may be when you reach a 'special birthday,' get married or divorced, contend with difficulties with a death of a loved one, and when you retire from a long-held job or profession.

Support is best when whoever supports you enables you to make your own decisions rather than imposing theirs onto you. Your ideal support is someone you can trust and talk to openly and not be judged by them. They should accept what you tell them without criticism so you can bounce ideas and discover what you need to do for yourself.

Is there somebody who can keep you on track? It could be a phone call to a friend or relative who asks how you are getting on.

Another way is to find a 'buddy' who wants to achieve something similar to you and who supports you if you support them.

If your mind is open to new ideas or goals, then finding someone to support you such as a coach or a mentor is useful to enable you to move forward and plan how to move on and discover how to renew your expectations about the future.

The secret for change is **positive thinking** by reflecting about good times. Bring those remembered emotions into the present and discover how to enjoy your situation more when you do this.

Notice how often you assume something can't happen or that you personally wouldn't be able to do something.

Rephrase your negative arguments into positive statements. These can become your affirmations: positive statements, said in the present tense, as if something you want is already happening.

Get involved in communities of which you are a part. Family, neighbours, friends, religious groups, creative groups, learning together, holidays, common activities are all communities in which to be involved, in a small or big way. Take part in local activities. Don't take things for granted. If something should change, then offer to do what is necessary.

Get in touch with your spiritual side. Spirituality is part of being who you are, whether you adhere to, or follow, a traditional religion. There is a connection with something outside of yourself that you may call God, Allah, The Universe, Higher self or anything else. Sometimes it's straightforward if you believe in the teachings of a particular religion. If you don't, then you may find there is a part of you that is as important as your physical being.

You may recognise this in nature, when you observe phenomena such as a beautiful sunrise or golden sunset. You may feel it when you see the power of the ocean and the waves crashing onto the cliffs or hear birds returning from their migration.

Whatever makes you aware of a power beyond yourself, connected with your purpose for being on Earth and is beyond your physical identity. The cycles of nature and the seasons can inspire and make you aware of something bigger than the self alone.

It's very common to go through a grieving reaction when you retire, because the transition involves loss and change. If you consider how much you will be 'giving up' when you retire and feel angry about the circumstances which led to having to, or needing to, retire, anger is one of the common reactions which people feel. You might feel guilty about what you are leaving for others to carry on with after you have left or some of the chaos you caused by not doing your work as efficiently as it could have been done. Most of all, you may feel very sad at leaving what has been a very important part of your life for very many years.

If any of these **emotions resonate,** then it is important to find the most suitable person or group to support you at a time of transition and change. You must decide what exactly you want. When you know this, you can seek the right person who can give that to you. Maybe you need informal or more formal support. Perhaps you need practical help with physical tasks or someone to talk to about your emotional or spiritual needs. You decide. When you know what you need, then ask for what you want specifically so the other person is able to respond to your request. It's no good just saying 'I want someone to help me,' because that may be interpreted as helping you in a completely different way.

Chapter 3 SELF CARE

Care for your body, mind and spirit. This means moving regularly, eating healthily, keeping your brain active by learning, reading, enquiring, and your spirit nurtured. Music, creativity or yoga can connect with these.

If you are changing your life, you need energy to do this. Make sure you eat and exercise regularly and healthily. Keep your brain active too by learning new things and being interested in the world around you, whatever your age.

If you are easily side-tracked, what might stop you making the changes you want? Interruptions may come as tasks which need doing, other people who decide what they want you to do, or make requests 'Now you are retired, could you just do so and so for me?'

Be certain about what you want to achieve, what outcome you want and, knowing the big picture, how much you can move towards your goal in the next week or in the next month.

When you have a plan, make it as a timetable so you have a routine for getting the job done. Decide how to deal with distractions, such as saying 'not now, but I can do it at such-and-such o'clock'? Then you will have time to do all the things you want to do.

Retirement is a time to rethink your daily routine and find new and exciting opportunities when you no longer have to keep to the work routine.

Plan for tomorrow, so you avoid waking up and wondering what to do. Keep note of events in the area you are interested in, or films or plays you want to see. When you decide the day before how to spend the next day, you will be excited to get on with your plans.

When you discover the joys of retirement and the wonderful opportunities to experience many new things, you will want to have a long retirement. Not only long but a healthy one too, to benefit from many years at this stage of your life.

Fitness is something to aim for as you get older and is a priority after retirement because this is a time in your life when past indiscretions come back to haunt you. Realise the healthy habits that you need to follow.

Perhaps you gave up smoking years ago, have experienced angina, or haven't taken enough exercise because you sat in your car for hours to go to meetings.

Start your '**get healthy**' campaign now. You know how important your health is, so commit to doing something about what you've neglected.

What are the most important things to do?

- *Keep muscles and joints flexible*
- *Eat healthily*
- *Drink alcohol in moderation*
- *Don't smoke*

Regular gentle exercise is vitally important. Walking is accessible to most people. If you want to do more, consider Yoga, Pilates, Tai Chi, dancing or golf. Keep moving, bending and stretching and you will slow down inevitable body changes that come with age because, as you get older, your body isn't able to do as much as it used to do.

Healthy habits may not be easy to maintain, especially at first, but if you persist, then you will have the benefits of remaining fit and well for longer, but it may take some perseverance until the habits become automatic and you do them without thinking.

What healthy habits do you need to develop?

If you want a long and happy retirement, then look after **your personal health and well-being.**

Improve your physical fitness by **regular exercise**. You have the advantage of senior rail cards and bus passes, if you live in the UK, so use these and enjoy visiting fresh places instead of driving. Using public transport more often also encourages you to walk more and thus benefits your health too.

Plan when, where, and what, so it happens. When you retire, you may either take on too many activities or not find the time to exercise or do nothing and sit around feeling sorry for yourself.

Resolve that you will do some exercise for at least half an hour on most days.

Developing new habits when you retire is important for enjoying your retirement and not being stressed.

Did you keep fit and healthy during your working years? Did the stress of the job mean good intentions fell by the wayside? Similarly, in retirement, you may intend to be healthy, but long-standing habits persist. However, if you persevere, you benefit by remaining fit and well for longer. Eventually, new habits become automatic and you do them without thinking.

Get your life more balanced. If your work was your life and you had no time for very little else, then something needs to change.

Eat food that is as natural form as possible, keeping a balance between the different food groups. These are: protein: meat, fish, eggs, beans, nuts, pulses and seeds and soya products such as tofu; complex carbohydrates: whole grains: wheat, barley, oats, corn, rice; and healthy fats: such as olive oil and coconut oil.

Keep your brain active by learning, reading and engaging in new hobbies and activities you wanted to try but never got around to while working long hours.

Chapter 4 LET GO OF STRESS

During your working life, you may have lived mostly in your head. Did you ever have time each day to 'switch off' from the worries and stress of your work? When you retire, you may at first find this switching off is something that you have to learn and find that you continue to worry about things which you can't do much about.

Connect with your breath because breathing slowly in and out while you count slowly to five is a way not only to relax but also to connect with your breath and a way to manage your stress levels. Breathe out stress and breathe in peace and relaxation.

Cut down caffeine which gives you the sense of having more energy, but this is a temporary energy boost. Caffeine makes your heart beat faster and can stop you sleeping at night but in moderation is beneficial.

Learn how to relax from head to toes for a few minutes each day by sitting comfortably and closing your eyes. Concentrate on thinking about each part of your body starting with your feet up to your head as you consciously tense that part and then let it go as you relax.

Go to bed earlier so you have enough sleep and start each new day refreshed. Avoid watching films before you go to bed that frighten you or drinking caffeine-containing drinks such as tea or coffee in the evening.

Take more aerobic exercise to keep your heart fit and your muscles working efficiently. Regular exercise will release endorphins into your bloodstream to help you feel relaxed, and regular exercise keeps your body fit and a healthy weight.

Do yoga to keep your body and mind flexible. Concentrating on the yoga postures leads to lowering of blood pressure and they have a calming effect so is an ideal pursuit for stress management.

Talk to someone about your stress because talking to a counsellor, therapist, coach, a friend or family member, someone who will listen and not judge you, to help you cope with the stress and discover ways to deal with it.

Share your household chores with the family or get paid help. When you are busy and feel stressed, let go of being perfect. If domestic chores take up a lot of your time, then either don't do them or delegate to other members of the household or pay for some help.

Allow extra time for journeys, so you avoid increased stress at the thought of being late for an appointment. Double the time you think it will take to get from A to B and arrive calm with time to spare.

Get involved in creative hobbies because creativity is a wonderful way to let go of stress. Being creative allows you to let go of day-to-day worries for a while as you engage in whatever creative activity you enjoy.

Get fitter physically and emotionally: Retirement offers an exciting opportunity for a new and interesting life. Avoid the temptation to sit around doing nothing except watching television and eating and drinking too much. It's vitally important to maintain a level of fitness in retirement years.

Chapter 5 DECISIONS

What do people do when they retire?

- *Travel*

- *Spend time with family and friends*

- *Pursue hobbies*

- *Volunteer*

- *Start a business*

- *Move to a new location*

- *Downsize their home*

- *Take up a new hobby*

Some people retire and immediately travel. Others stay home and focus on spending time with family and friends. Several people get part-time jobs or volunteer. Others spend their retirement learning new things and keeping their minds active, yet more relax and enjoy not having to work anymore.

Travel the world: You've left your job and decide to go on a world tour or a cruise. When you retire, the world can be your oyster and the only restriction will be how much money you want to spend.

Clear the clutter: Eventually you come down to earth and look around your home environment and see that you have accumulated a vast array of things some of which have sentimental value, some are still useful and many of their things are neither wanted, nor loved. You come to terms with clearing away the latter and making space both physically and emotionally.

Be more aware of the source of clutter coming into your life and get rid of old journals and magazines, photos and clothes that will never fit you again or are for a different lifestyle: office suits have little use when they live the more relaxed lifestyle of a retired person.

Clear clutter: because when you retire from work, you have the chance to sort through and dispose of work-related things.

Throw away lots. One reason for your disorganisation may be because you have too much 'stuff.' Be ruthless and dispose of anything out of date, such as journals, papers, old statements, clothes, and food. Recycle or compost what you can and take usable household goods and clothes to a charity shop.

Clear your desk completely, then sort and tidy as you put things back. Choose a surface or a drawer or cupboard, then put what you need back on or into it, considering whether to keep or dispose of each item.

Place objects into categories. Stop your desk or office being a jumble of things, and store like with like.

When you have an efficient system, you can find things more easily. Discover what would work best for you. A traditional filing cabinet works well so long as you can put your paperwork into files labelled by subject. You may prefer document trays or boxes or become paper-less and store everything on your computer.

Set yourself a time limit for each task. Tasks expand to fill an enormous amount of time. If you put a bit of pressure on yourself to finish something within a limited time, or at least do as much of it as you can, it will amaze you at how much you achieve.

Keep up to date with paying bills and your accounts. Don't delay paying your bills. Either set up direct debit arrangements to pay recurring expenses or pay as soon as you receive the bill. Similarly, keep up to date with your accounts and credit card payments.

Limit the time you spend surfing the internet. Keep focused on your internet searches. The internet has become a vital tool for research and information gathering.

Make it a routine to **check emails** at certain times of the day. Set up folders to filter emails out of your main inbox. Unsubscribe from as many emails which you don't have the time to read.

Make a pile of old paperwork, and deal with some each day. Spend some time dealing with it, rather than new stuff, which goes into a different pile.

While you **deliberate about deciding**, be clear of what your choices, because things aren't just a matter of A or B, there may be a midway choice which can be a compromise that you hadn't considered before.

If you seem to have an enormous number of choices, start by **grouping them together as broad solutions** rather than being very specific at this stage. You will be better able to narrow your choice, and you can chunk down into smaller choices and into greater specifics about exactly what you want to do. Ask yourself what you need to find out or learn about before you make the final decision.

Make a list of pros and cons. Making a list of the good things of each is a way to decide, and it means that you make an informed choice. However, not everyone decides in that way: some will ask around and get the opinions of others who have experienced something similar, while others go by their instinct about what is the right thing to do. Most of us use a bit of each in varying degrees.

Notice your internal voice. Write each pro and con if you are someone who decides on your internal feelings about something. Notice as you write each word how you feel slightly different. Using this aspect of your physiology enables you to assess what choice to make.

Go along with your 'gut feeling' about the right choice helps you choose as much as any other parameter such as hearing what people say about what you want to do, or looking at photos or objects connected with what you plan. Each of these are ways in which people decide. We tend to use a bit of each, but many of us have a preference.

Consider alternatives. Prepare a Plan B if your primary choice goes completely wrong. Although you can't be sure the choice you make will turn out to be the best choice, it is re-assuring to know that if your first choice fails you can fall back on another choice.

Prepare well. Assuming you have finally made a choice referred to as Plan A, then be as prepared for all eventualities as you can. Prepare more detail for your plan A: is there anything you need to find out before you can be sure it's right for you?

Chapter 6 CHALLENGES

Get your boundaries clear: don't expect others to be mind-readers. Don't be frustrated if others misunderstand what you want them to do: maybe you've made assumptions and haven't been really clear about what you are expecting from them.

Decide what you really want. When you know what it is, then you will be more able to tell others and no longer have to put up with unsatisfactory performance.

Communicate clearly. Give a positive feedback sandwich if you are not happy with the way someone is behaving. Say something complimentary then get to what it is you want, finally end on something positive.

Be responsible for yourself. Do not avoid making changes because you think it will upset someone. Tell them what you are going to do and when, then allow them the chance to deal with it in their own way.

Improve your self-care. Stop neglecting your own needs for your body, mind and spirit in whatever ways are good for you. You may have looked forward to retiring from work because your job was tiring, stressful without time to do anything else. During the working day, you used both physical and emotional, energy so you only wanted to eat your meal and have an early night.

There is no work routine: At first it may excite you that the day is your own, but this is a test if you are at the end of a working life filled with routine and knew exactly what you would do each day. Even keeping track of the day of the week can be a challenge because you may not have activities linked to a certain day.

It is you who has to **organise your day** rather than your boss or manager and you haven't yet got into the habit of exploring different activities.

Keep your mind active: You can read all those books you never had the time for in the past, joining a class or two to get up to date with computers and the internet, or join a club that meets socially and has regular informative talks.

It's easy to become lazy: It seems tempting at first to do very little and become a couch potato, but you can overcome this by involvement in extra activities. You'll make new friends, learn new skills, and find ways to spend your days. You'll do many of those things you promised yourself that you would do when you retired.

When you are used to someone else telling you what to do, it can be a test to make your own choices, but you'll get used to it. Make the effort and this will become part of your new routine as you become used to the challenges of retirement and enjoy your new life phase.

Other people think you have all the time in the world: They see you as someone retired and no longer working, so may ask you to do things for them. You might find these requests rather difficult to deal with because you want to help others yet are not used to saying no to them because you may believe your reasons for not wanting to do things for others is selfish on your part.

When you retire, it is important to decide **how to spend your time** so you don't waste your precious days. Of course, there is a balance to be struck between enjoying your greater leisure time and aimlessly passing the days doing very little at all.

Begin with the end in mind.

Stephan Covey

However, you may find that once the pressures of work are no longer on you, you **don't get things done** as quickly as you did before you retired and you do more **leisure-based activities** than before.

Make plans and develop a big vision of what you would like to achieve as you don't have to conform to the pressures of work because when you know what you want, you can think about what might stop you succeeding and whether there are valid objections to your success.

Perhaps you want to write a book, or learn a foreign language, or travel to fresh places. If so, make choices about what to do first, find out what you need to start those projects and then take those first steps.

Although it's important to **listen to other people's opinions** about what you hope to do, especially those people who are nearest and dearest, don't take all their objections to heart. Find **those who encourage you** to go forward with what you want to do and get their opinions too.

Trust your intuition about whether something is right for you and if there are genuine reasons, why you wouldn't be able to have a go at what you want to do. You can be very active and do so many things, so get going with them while you have time and energy on your side.

Chapter 7 WHAT TO DO?

Find a balance between doing nothing and doing too much: Remember that your energy levels may not be as high as they were years ago, but don't let your biological age put you off the activity which you want to do.

What have you always wanted to learn? You can discover whether there are courses, so you can spend some valuable time improving your skills.

Decide what physical activities you like. This is a good time to swim regularly, attend exercise classes, practice Yoga or Tai chi, or ride your bicycle every day. Pick two or three and explore these. Decide whether you can do them on your own or if you need a companion or a class, and plan your week.

Avoid getting stressed by things you can't influence, have fun, try new things, make friends and laugh every day. There is no advantage in being stressed because retirement is a time to enjoy life, learn new skills and reflect on all the things that have brought you to where you find yourself now.

Whatever you dream of, **make the plan**, mark the steps in your diary and then **take action**. If it's an enormous project, plan and make your own deadline and schedule to follow. Take it one step at a time; remembering your steps can be as big or as small as you wish, as long as you take them so you will move forward into the life you want. Having a sense of humour is optional, but it helps!

Learn new ways to do things. You have many skills in relation to your work and life. Now you can adapt these and have fun exploring and learning fresh ways too. Perhaps there are specific skills you want to learn. Find out about your local adult education centre and what they offer.

It's very rewarding at the end of a long career to **mentor others** who are starting out. Find out about the University of the Third Age (u3a) and how you can learn and teach others, because teaching is as useful as learning. As you teach, you also learn. The questions they ask you will make you aware of how things change and might make you come to terms with the fact that it really was time to retire. Now is also the time to **develop talents** kept suppressed for years.

Perhaps you've hidden your **creative abilities**. If so, pick up a paintbrush or a piece of charcoal and find out what happens. If you've always wanted to write poetry or a novel, get started, let the ideas flow. You can learn the basics and meet others with the same passions, then explore your creativity to the full.

Plan your days, your week, and your month. Not rigidly like a work schedule, but in a fluid way that allows some flexibility.

Don't become a couch potato. It may be a temptation when you no longer have the routine of work to sit around and watch television and eat crisps all day, but this isn't the way to have a rewarding life after work. What you have to do now that you have the time to plan your days is to connect with your passion and with the enthusiasm you get from thinking about what fires you up, excites and motivates you.

Devise a strategy: step by manageable step to take, to move from where you are now to where you want to be. Remember, it's not the ultimate achievement; it's working out how you can make the shift from here to there and the steps to take. When you do this, you won't be lazy anymore because your excitement gives you the energy to shift yourself forward and achieve what you want. You'll be able to do this by **letting go of things** that you no longer have to do now. Share tasks with your partner or other members of your family. Tell them you won't be so available in the future.

Prioritise what you have to do so you don't become overwhelmed. You don't have to do everything, but decide what is vital today. Eliminate your time-wasters. You may choose to spend some of your day doing things such as watching television, when there are other more important things to do.

Notice what distracts you from your task and take steps about how you can deal with this another time. Does your neighbour come around uninvited and expect coffee and a chat? Explain that it's not always convenient and suggest a time better for you.

- *Make a timetable, so you have a rough idea what you plan to do each day.*

- *Divide your time between different tasks so you can vary what you do.*

- *Do something physical then something sitting at your computer.*

- *You don't have to finish one task completely before you do part of another. Because the very process of starting something makes it easier to return to it later and continue where you left off.*

When you know what you want and are passionate about it, then you can find the time to take the steps.

The big goal, the vision and your purpose will all drive your motivation and enable you to look at what options you have to reach your goal. If you feel stuck, or lacking in motivation to proceed, or if you feel disheartened by people cynical about your ability to reach your goal.

If you use the excuse of not having the time to do something which would move you towards the life you want, then think again.

Perhaps you need to **reconsider what you want**, then relax and brainstorm as many ideas as possible about other ways to move forward. Strange though it may seem, if you keep asking yourself 'what other ways could I achieve that?' you will come up with lots of other ways. Once you gain clarity, you will have the motivation to take the steps you need to take.

When you move out of your old life and into a new one to have a life after work, **opportunities will inspire and motivate you.**

Dream as you've done for years, but you are almost there when it becomes your reality. Are you ready to take the vision out of your head and your imagination and into the world outside? Are you ready to let others know what it is you've been longing for during those years of work when it was thoughts about retirement and what you could do that kept you going through hours of business or of boredom?

Now is the time for your ideas to take precedence. No managers or government targets to reach. No work-related deadlines anymore. You are your own boss and you can do whatever you want.

You have the ideas, now make a plan in order to put them into reality. You may need deadlines and be accountable and decide by when you want to achieve and to whom you will be accountable.

Set a realistic date by when you want to achieve the entire dream and then break it down into smaller chunks so that week by week you can achieve sensible amounts. Plan what you will do each day to move the dream nearer to achievement. Then bit-by-bit things happen. Even five or ten minutes each day will move things forward. Many people find this is a more effective way to make progress than planning to do a tremendous amount in one day. A small bit of several jobs each day is a preference. You can try changing activities every half an hour from sitting still to moving around.

You may find allotting an entire day to something suits your personality. That's fine, so long as you actually do that. Too many people have the intention but never have the full day to assign to one task.

Chapter 8 RELATIONSHIPS

As we age, our relationships change. Some of our friends move away, some pass away, and some simply drift out of our lives. At the same time, we may find ourselves spending more time with our spouses, children, and grandchildren. Retirement can be a time of great joy as we enjoy our relationships more fully.

However, retirement can also be a time of great loneliness. As our social circles shrink, we can feel isolated and cut off from the world. It's important to stay connected to others, whether it's through online communities, volunteering, or simply staying in touch with old friends.

No matter what our situation, retirement can be a time to cherish our relationships. Whether we're spending more time with our loved ones or reaching out to new friends, retirement can be a wonderful time to enjoy the company of those we care about.

Relationships and friendships are important at all stages of your life. As you move into an unknown part of life, you find changes because it's a time to move on and let go. Some friendships are solid and continue throughout life, while others need to be left behind. Perhaps those friends you had while you were at work will no longer have the connection you had before. Yet there are new friends with the fresh interests and activities you engage in. It may be a challenge to make completely new friends.

Close relationship with your wife, husband or partner, change too on retirement and are a potential cause of stress. You need to respect each other's need for space, both physical and emotional. Unless you worked together, when you retire you will be in each other's company for far longer than you have been for years. It's a time to get to know each other again, and to come to terms with your different interests, so you have time together and time apart, too.

Some people find that their relationships change in retirement, while others find that their relationships stay the same.

Some people find that they have more time for their friends and family in retirement, while others find that they have less time.

Some people find that they are able to travel more in retirement, while others find that they are not able to travel as much.

Some people find that their relationships with their children change in retirement, while others find that their relationships with their children stay the same.

Chapter 9 GENERAL ADVICE

What are you planning to do differently during your retirement? When you reach the time to retire, look at your life from the outside and re-assess where you want it to take you from now onwards. Your life involves others, not just you, so whatever you wish to do may affect not only you but also your partner, your friends, family, and your community.

What you decide to do after you let go of the work routine is, to a large extent, up to you. We may relate it to a long-forgotten hobby which you wish to take up again or pursue other interests which you had no time to take part in when you were busy at work. You know, as you get older, that your health and well-being become even more important, and this is the time to look at your lifestyle in relation to your state of health and wellness, deciding what you must do now to increase your chances of a healthy old age.

There is nothing to stop you from doing what you wish you'd done years ago.

Many people decide to apply for jobs in a completely different industry, or start their own business, possibly working from home.

Quality of life is important, and it starts with your environment. If you've always wanted to live somewhere different, now is the time to make the move. Environment affects the way you view life. What difference does it make to you when you hear the screech of seagulls or waves crashing on the shore compared with the hum of motorway traffic or the judder of brakes at a main road junction? It's different for everyone.

If the place is where you are now, then now may be the time to **clear away your accumulated clutter**, so you surround yourself with things you love. Whatever you prefer when you choose where to live, remember to consider both the big picture and also the smaller. Something as simple as changing the ornaments on a shelf may have a positive effect on the way you feel about life. Does your room need decorating? Adjust the colour on the walls and you transform your view of life, too. Throw away the clothes you'll never get into again and you'll have the space to gain a new image for the next stage in your life. When the outside pleases you, your inside will delight you, too.

Visualise what your life will look like when you achieve these. In your mind, hear the positive reactions of others when you succeed and notice how you feel when you know you are doing what you love to do. Do the visualisation every day. The best times are just as you wake or as you fall asleep at night. Get yourself prepared in this way to step into your new life because when you do this regularly, then your subconscious mind enables you to make the adjustments to eventually being able to achieve what you really want during your retirement years.

Have a balance between all parts of your life. Remember how important it is to address those things that make you into a whole person. It's vital to communicate and relate to others, your partner, friends and family. Make regular connections with your friends, those you have now and some from the past who you have lost touch with, and family too. Make sure you speak on the telephone and visit often.

Spend time with your family. Love them or hate them, they are part of you and your life. Families come together even when separated by country or continent, to celebrate with ritual to mark a transition such as birth, marriage or death.

Spend time with friends You choose your friends whereas you inherit your family. You are friends with those with whom you have common interests. Keep friendships alive by making contact regularly, even if you can't meet face to face.

Spend time with your partner to keep your relationship alive. It's important to have time together and also time apart to do those things that interest you.

Don't neglect your own interests and hobbies. However, as much as you enjoy being with your partner, friends or family, it's most important to address your own needs for relaxation and enjoyment and maintain an interest in hobbies and recreation.

Don't take life too seriously. Make sure you find something to laugh about each day. Laughter helps to relax you, and when you see the funny side of a situation, it can also seem less stressful. Read an amusing book, see a funny film, or just tell stories about what happened in a way to make people laugh.

Confidence and self-belief are two ingredients needed to make alternative choices when you retire. If one or other of these is missing, then you may find that life plods on with little positive improvement. To open the doors of your new life, you must nurture a belief that you can achieve the transformation you hope for and you need to check that you have the ability, whether this is physical, or emotional, to look at life through new eyes, and also the persistence to keep on trying even if things don't work out the way you want them to at first.

Remember that rather than failure, there is some **learning from every experience**. Don't give up. Observe how a toddler learns to walk. Do they give up on the first fall? No, they get up and try to walk yet fall again and again until they finally are able to walk.

Chapter 10 CONFIDENCE

Do you wish you were more confident? Affirmations can help. Compose short positive statements in the present tense, beginning with 'I am....' stating whatever it is you want to achieve as though you have already succeeded. Then repeat these in your head all day hundreds of times so that your subconscious mind believes they are true.

You may feel apprehensive about what you will do with yourself each day when you no longer go to work, or you may be glad to be rid of the job you didn't enjoy.

Do things you really love: There is no point at all in doing things that bore you or you don't enjoy. Of course, there may be different levels of enjoyment, but overall if you don't like it then stop doing it.

Avoid doing things solely because someone else asked you. When you retire, people assume you have all the time in the world and don't know how to fill those hours. Say 'yes' to what you want and 'no' to the rest.

Spend time with people whose company you enjoy: It's not like having a job, being retired means you can choose not only what you do but also who to do it with. Stop putting up with those people you don't like and spend more time with those whose company you enjoy.

Learn something: Keep your brain active in retirement by acquiring new skills whether these are learning a language, becoming more efficient with computer skills or playing a musical instrument. Whatever it is, choose something you enjoy or look forward to doing.

Try something new: If you don't want to attend a long course, look out for study days, or taster sessions of different activities so that you can experience new things and decide if you want to pursue them more.

Take part in activities that stretch your body or your mind or your spiritual experience of life. Learning about other people's view of the world helps to keep you young.

There may be **activities you wish you'd done years ago** and might include travel to countries you've not visited before, learning a foreign language or a musical instrument, or taking up a sport which you've wanted to try but not had the courage to do so before you retired. Lifelong learning is important, so keep your mind and body as active as possible.

Do what you've always wanted to do because retirement is the time to finish projects you started years ago, get your clutter sorted at last and do things you didn't get around to before. Maybe you always wanted to travel and see other parts of the world. Make your plans and achieve them now.

Are all your **long-learned skills** from many years in your working environment wasted once you retire? People refer to 'transferable skills.' This means you may not use them in precisely the same way as you did before, but there may be ways you can apply some to your life now. For example, how did you organise your day, your workspace, or your life to fit in all that you needed to do each day? Can you apply those skills to your life now so you can get on with things but without the overwhelm and stress of the work environment?

You can devise systems for **getting things done** in relation to your self-care, your household tasks, your hobbies, your friends, family and community, and your partner. When you retire, you must make a shift in your work-life balance, away from the stress of a job and towards the life you want now. Allow yourself more time for relaxation and also for moving your projects forward.

Chapter 11 GOAL SETTING

Some people don't think you need to set goals because they like to do whatever takes their fancy and not have to do certain things. This is a great philosophy of life, but it may not result in getting specific things accomplished.

An enormous challenge for many people is 'getting things done'. Do you jump from one thing to another and eventually realise that it achieves very little with this approach? By setting specific goals and being very clear about the steps you have to take to achieve what you want, progress towards your goal is phenomenally faster than if you flit from task to task with little in mind as the end product.

Set yourself clear goals you wish to work towards. Visualise what your life will look like when you achieve these. Listen to the positive reactions of others when you succeed and notice how you feel when you know you are doing what you love to do. Do the visualisation every day without fail. The best times are just as you wake or as you fall asleep at night. Get yourself prepared in this way to step into your new life because when you do this regularly, your subconscious mind enables you to make the adjustments to being able to achieve what you really want during your retirement years.

Keep your mind focussed instead of moving from task to task with little progress, knowing the goal you so it's more likely to have the outcome you want.

Break down big goals into smaller steps because what you want to achieve may be more than you can do in one session, so you have to plan the steps you need to take to get to where you want to go.

Take action because you have goals, instead of not doing much and thinking that what you really want is too big for you to achieve.

Goals clarify what you want specifically and by when you want to achieve, so you take the actions.

You get a great sense of satisfaction and cause for celebration when you reach your goals because when you realise you can achieve your confidence expands so tyou not only set more goals but also set them higher than before. There is always a personal challenge.

It's important to achieve something regularly. In order to do this, you must set goals which are realistic and achievable bearing in mind your age, ability and personal situation. You won't get that sense of satisfaction when a goal is too high to be a realistic goal for you to attain.

Balance setting goals which are too easy and don't give that same sense of achievement with goals which are a challenge. You may feel despondent because you feel that your previous success has taken a turn for the worse and wonder what to do to get back on track and turn around the negative impact your drop in success is having on you.

There has to be a balance between what you do for yourself and what you do because of pressure from others. If you can, balance both demands on your time and energy. However, if not, be aware of your own internal reactions to doing those things you love to do against doing something because of an obligation. If the latter leaves you feeling drained or stressed, then it is very important to confront this and make adjustments so that whatever you do gives you a feeling of excitement and anticipation.

Success may not last forever, so you will need to accept the effect of change and be able to deal with the emotions that brings.

Re-assess what you want to achieve.

The world changes and maybe whatever you were successful in doing is now more commonplace, so there are more people offering the same as you and your offering is no longer needed in its original format. Ask yourself what you want to achieve. It may differ from when you were successful in the past.

Take a break to increase your motivation.

If you feel stuck in trying to achieve something that no longer is successful for you, then it's useful to take a holiday in order to relax, let go of any frustration and stress, and to allow new ideas to filter through to you. You will return with new ideas about what to do from now onwards.

Visualise your life when you achieve these. Listen to the positive reactions of others when you succeed and notice how you feel when you know you are doing what you love to do. The best times are just as you wake or as you fall asleep at night. Get yourself prepared in this way to step into your new life because when you do this regularly, your subconscious mind enables you to make the adjustments to being able to achieve what you really want during your retirement years.

Achieve your goals. If nothing changes because you haven't decided what you want, then look to the future and decide to take action instead thinking about what you don't want.

Set specific goals and a time frame. Then take the first steps. When you decide your outcome, choose how you will know when you've achieved this. It helps if there is a specific way to decide this rather than a vague phrase like 'I'll be happier'

Imagine yourself being projected into your future life when you've achieved what you want and look back on yourself now. Tell the present you what to do differently to enable you to achieve what you want.

Chapter 12 LET GO OF STRESS

"The thought of retirement fills me with dread. I don't know how I'm going to fill my days, or how I'm going to afford to live on a fixed income. I worry that I'll be bored and lonely, and that my health will decline. I'm not sure I'm ready to give up my work identity, or my sense of purpose. I don't know if I can handle not being needed anymore."

How you decide to fill your retirement time is up to you, but initially you need to make a shift in your mind-set about what you do now that you no longer fill your day with work.

If you are someone who has spent most of your life doing things for others, then deciding what you would really like for yourself might be a challenge. However, if you love caring for others but your day seems empty without work, then you could look in your local paper. There are usually opportunities for volunteers who want to care for others less able than themselves. These people might be disabled or recovering from an illness and need someone to do some odd jobs for them or just call in for a chat regularly. You might like to clear some beaches or build a wall or two and open your eyes to the various opportunities available.

Once you take a bit of time to get used to the idea of not going to work, you might instead want to pursue a learning opportunity to get to grips with a subject you've always been interested in yet never had the time to learn about.

Perhaps you've always wanted to travel, and the first step to doing this might be to learn the language of that country. Don't despair and think you'll be bored when you retire. There is a wealth of things to do or get involved in. Some may involve you spending some of your pension, whereas others might be employment so you can increase your income.

During your working life, you may have lived mostly in your head. Did you ever have time each day to 'switch off' from the worries and stress of your work?

When you retire, you may at first find this switching off is something that you have to learn and find that you continue to worry about things which you can't do much about.

There are two habits to develop when you retire in relation to enjoying your retirement and not getting stressed.

Exercise and relax regularly. Whatever your age of physical ability, you will benefit from exercise. It doesn't have to be high powered. In fact, the best forms of exercise, whatever your age, are: walking, swimming, dancing or yoga or a combination of these. The most important things are that it is regularly that you can do it and that you enjoy yourself.

You need to plan when, where and what so that it happens. The trouble is that when you retire you may either take on too many activities or not find the time to exercise 0or do nothing and sit around feeling sorry for yourself.

Resolve that you will do some exercise for at least half an hour on most days. The easiest is to go out of your front door and walk.

If you want to be with others, then you could have a walk with someone or find out about local classes, whether these are for exercise at your local gym or for class activities such as dancing or yoga. Yoga is beneficial, as you get older, because you can do it even if you have a disability. Not only that, but whatever your age, yoga will keep your muscles and joints flexible and also your mind.

After you have done some exercise, make sure you also relax. This can be done sitting in a chair or lying down for a few minutes. Think about each part of your body and tense and then relax it from your feet to your head and as you do this think about letting go of tension and allowing the muscles to relax. Then let everything be completely relaxed for a few moments as you breathe in and out slowly and allow your body to recover from the exercise.

It's so important to **care for your body, mind and spirit**. This means moving regularly, eating healthily, keeping your brain active by learning and reading and enquiring, and your spirit too by connecting with your inner self or Higher Being, or God, according to your own beliefs. Music, creativity or yoga can connect with these. If you are changing your life, you need to have the energy to do this. Make sure you eat and exercise regularly and healthily. Keep your brain active too by learning new things and being interested in the world around you, whatever your age.

What diversions, if you are easily side-tracked, might stop you making the changes you want for your retirement? They may come as other tasks which need doing, other people who decide what is best for you, or make requests of you in 'Now you have retired, could you just do so and so for me?' You need to be very clear about what it is you want to achieve, and about what outcome you want and, knowing the big picture, you must be clear about how much you can move yourself towards your goal in the next week or in the next month.

When you have a plan, make it as a timetable so you will have a routine for getting the job done. You will decide how to deal with distractions, such as saying 'not now, but I can do it at such-and-such o'clock' Then you will have time to do all the things you want to do.

During your working life, you may have lived mostly in your head. Did you ever have time each day to 'switch off' from the worries and stress of your work? When you retire, you may at first find this switching off is something that you have to learn and find that you continue to worry about things which you can't do much about.

Connect with your breath because breathing slowly in and out while you count slowly to five is a way not only to relax but also to connect with your breath and a way to manage your stress levels. Breathe out stress and breathe in peace and relaxation.

Cut down caffeine, which gives you the sense of having more energy, but in fact this is a temporary energy boost. Caffeine makes your heart beat faster and can stop you from sleeping at night.

Learn how to relax from head to toes for a few minutes each day by sitting comfortably and closing your eyes. Concentrate on thinking about each part of your body, starting with your feet up to your head as you consciously tense that part and then let it go as you relax.

Go to bed earlier so you have enough sleep and start each new day refreshed. Avoid watching films before you go to bed that frighten you or drinking caffeine-containing drinks such as tea or coffee.

Take more aerobic exercise to keep your heart fit and your muscles working efficiently. Regular exercise will release endorphins into your bloodstream to help you feel relaxed, and regular exercise keeps your body fit and a healthy weight.

Do yoga to keep your body and mind flexible. By concentrating on the yoga postures leads to lowering of blood pressure and they have a calming effect so is an ideal pursuit for stress management.

Talk to someone about your stress because talking to a counsellor, therapist or coach or to a friend or family member, someone who will listen and not judge you, is very beneficial to help you cope with the stress and work out ways to deal with it.

Share your household chores with the family or get paid help. When you are very busy and feel stressed, you must let go of 'being perfect' If domestic chores take up a lot of your time, then either don't do them or delegate to other members of the household or pay for some help.

Allow extra time for journeys, so you avoid increased stress at the thought of being late for an appointment. Double the time you think it will take to get from A to B and arrive calm with time to spare.

Chapter 13 BE RETIRED

Some people love being retired, yet others get extremely fed up after some time they miss the comradeship of work and the routine they had.

Here are some ways that **you can become even more fed up and frustrated** when you retire.

Don't plan what you are going to do when you retire. Maybe you believe you will automatically know how to spend your day when you retire. However, after a lifetime of work routine, you may find it's quite difficult to decide what to do each day. Before you know it, days, weeks, months and finally years pass and you know that you've wasted a lot of time.

Give up. Decide your life is over, so no point in doing anything new. However, it's not too late to make plans about what you'll do during your retirement. You could follow where your spirit leads you, but may find that unless you make plans, it is more likely that you will become more and more fed up.

Only have friends who are connected to your workplace. You may find that all your friends are people who worked with you. That means that your friendship is related to sharing what goes on at work. So when you leave you find that, with time, you have less and less in common and this is a formula for becoming more and more frustrated and bored.

Instead, you could start by joining clubs, going to adult education classes and meeting new people not connected with your working life.

Never take time to learn anything different. You can guarantee that you will become more and more fed up during retirement if you have learnt nothing about life except for things you had to learn in relation to your work. Find out what classes there are and open your mind to new opportunities.

Don't have hobbies. By spending all your time at work, you will have perfected the art of not doing anything else except working, watching television, eating and sleeping. This is the perfect formula for being very fed up once you are retired.

Remember what you used to enjoy and promise yourself that you will find others so you make new friends and keep your mind and body active?

When you leave employment and start a new life, and wonder how to fill your days, or discover that there is so much to do that you do not have sufficient time to do what you planned to accomplish during your retirement. Can you ensure you use your time to do enough, yet still can relax and reflect?

What have you always wanted to do? During your retirement you have at a chance to fulfil the dreams you had all your life. Make a list of them on a separate piece of paper for each one and record what you have to do in order to do those tasks.

What is your legacy? When you retire, you think about growing older and the inevitability of dying. How do you want people to remember you? What would you leave behind when you are no longer here? When you think about the answers to these questions, you may become more aware of what you have to do during your retirement.

What do you have to do to start? If you know what you want to do, then the important thing is to take action. Sometimes, that is the most difficult step to take. You may have set yourself a step too large so ask yourself 'what do I have to do before I can do that?' and keep asking that question until you decide on something that will only take you a few moments and that you can do right now. It's amazing how quickly you move to the next and the next step once you have taken that first step.

Becoming a retired person. It may happen, however, because you have retired that other people believe you are at their beck and call and will do anything they ask of you. It's important that you are aware of this possibility and that you do what you want to do for others, but not so much that you no longer have the time to follow your own interests and hobbies.

Think about how you want to spend your days when retired. You no longer have to go to work each day, so be careful of filling your day with other obligations that you don't want. You may be a person who only wants to do those things for other people and is happy to be of use to them. That is fine, so long as you are not avoiding the possibility of doing new and exciting things, too.

When they ask you to do something, consider if you want to say 'yes' or 'no'. If you decide to help, then be clear with that person whether they believe you are promising to doing this every day, or regularly. Do you want that commitment?

It might be a relief to have something to do. You might resent your agreement if new opportunities come your way for other things. Being retired is a lot about finding a balance between your obligations to others and obligations to yourself. That's why it's important to spend a bit of time sorting these in your own mind to clarify how to respond to others who want to use your time and energy and which might cause you having less of both to use for your personal retirement projects.

It's not a matter of all or nothing. There is a middle way when you can do things for others and spend part of your day in doing those things but also having plenty of time, energy and motivation for yourself.

Do you have ample energy? You are entering a significant journey for a new stage of life and you need to have not only plans but also the motivation and be willing to get up and change those things you want to change.

Life is a tremendous adventure, and you may be about to have the biggest ride of all. When you begin, recognise the possibilities and opportunities that are there for you now. Keep calm and acknowledge the excitement you feel. Work out plans and a timetable for what you want to do. You need to brush away the objections that may surface in your own mind and speak to others. You must keep calm, decide what you want, develop your vision and the steps to achieve it. Have a time frame to act like a work-place target. Most people find that working to a deadline is motivating for getting things done.

When you identify what you want, what might stop you from succeeding? Decide how you can get rid of as many obstacles as possible and clarify what your very first step must be. When you take that first step, you will be on your way to having the life you want.

There are many ways to get yourself and your life more organised. This is important when you retire. Retirement brings you many new opportunities, so if you are wasting time regularly, then you need to find how to use your day more efficiently and effectively to fulfill some or all of your long-held ambitions and also explore new possibilities to enjoy life.

Plan your day the previous evening. This is one way to get more order into your life. However, if you don't like an imposed schedule, which may bring back memories of working with tight demands on your time, you may prefer to greet each day anew with a little idea at the start of it where it and your spirit will lead you.

However, it's worth trying and noticing how much more you can achieve each day. It can be a great motivator when you spend a few moments each evening thinking about and then deciding about what you want to get done the following day.

Be realistic. You know what you can do, so set yourself tasks which you know you can easily complete in the time you have available. It's important to be realistic about this.

Be specific. Avoid being vague about what you want to do. Rather than deciding something like 'continue with clearing clutter,' try instead to specify precisely what you will get done.

Write it down. The other important thing to remember is to make a note about whatever you decide to do. The mere act of writing something merges it in your mind, and you will be much more likely to do it.

Strike a balance. Be aware of aiming too high or aiming too low when deciding what you want to get done the following day. When you aim too low, you can always do more and so feel very pleased with yourself, whereas aiming too high can lead you to feel frustrated and as if you have failed.

Designate specific times for yourself. You may have had years of too little exercise and eating unhealthy food during your working life. Don't let your increased leisure time lead you to eating more and exercising less. Take the opportunities you have to increase your health and well-being.

Don't be bored. Not going to work anymore and beginning to feel bored with not having a routine? Here are some ways that you can prevent boredom during retirement.

For most people, retirement turns out to be a very exciting time with little opportunity for boredom. It is more often a fear that people have before they've actually retired. However, you may find that being bored after you retire is a real possibility, especially if you find it difficult to let go of your working identity.

It is important to understand that retirement is a new stage of your life. There may be a period of transition from your life as someone who goes out to work every day to your life as a retired person.

Inevitably, you will develop a new identity when you retire. Yes, part of you is the same as it was before, but a large part of you changes and this is something you may need to work at.

Since retirement is an opportunity to explore new ways of living your life, then it is also a chance to gradually change the way you view what's happening around you.

Things that used to be overwhelmingly important take on a lesser significance after you've retired. You may wonder why you put up with so many things during your working life and understand how important other aspects of life are.

These may be to do with your family and friends, becoming more involved in community activities, and also doing things for yourself, whether pursuing hobbies long since forgotten, or being more aware about how important it is to look after your own health and well-being.

So stopping being bored when you retire you must take an active role and decide what it is you really would like to do now that you no longer have work commitments, because until you decide what it is you want then it will be more difficult to achieve it. Once you've decided what you'd like to spend your time doing, then make the plans to actually do it.

Find out about local facilities and classes in your area that are related to the things you'd like to do. Sometimes you can't jump from your working persona into a new identity without learning something new. In fact, learning at this time of your life is very exciting. It keeps your brain active and ensures that you will not be bored during retirement.

When you retire, the biggest problem you meet is there is too much choice about what you can do.

When you retire from work and become a 'retired person', you may wonder how you are going to fill your days, or find that there is so much to do that you hardly have enough time to do what you planned to do during your retirement.

What can you do to ensure that you don't waste your time and yet have enough time to do plenty yet also can relax and reflect?

At first, you think you will be bored when you haven't got enough to do because you no longer have the routine of work. You believe it will be difficult to fill your day with useful activities.

However, the truth is there are a huge number of things you can do when you no longer have to work.

The challenge may decide which of those things you are going to do.

If you have such a problem with that decision, you could end up either hardly doing anything or doing far too much and becoming exhausted.

Here is what to do to help solve this problem:

Write about all the things you really love doing. Ask yourself: what have you always wanted to learn about? You can research whether there are courses you could enroll in so that you can spend some valuable time improving your skills.

What have you always wanted to do? During your retirement, you have at a chance to fulfill the dreams you had all your life. Make a list of them, on a separate piece of paper for each one, and write what you have to do in order to achieve those things.

Decide what physical activities you like taking part in. This is a good time to plan to swim regularly, attend exercise classes, practice Yoga or T'ai chi, or ride your bicycle every day.

From the list that you've made, pick two or three and explore these. Decide which day or days you will do those things, whether you can do them on your own or if you need to find a companion or a class, and plan your week.

Find a balance between doing nothing and doing too much. Remember that your energy levels may not be as high as they were years ago, but on the other hand, don't let your biological age put you off the activity which you want to do.

See the funny side of life. Avoid getting stressed by things which you can't influence, have fun, try new things, make friends and be sure you laugh every day. There is no advantage in getting overstressed because your retirement is a time to enjoy life, learn new skills and reflect on all the things that have brought you to where you find yourself now.

Chapter 14 STOP DREADING IT

Does the thought of retirement fill you with dread, especially if you have got into a habit of not going out except to work and visiting friends?

You may be anxious about how to fill your days once retired and even if you have plenty to do, there are a lot of hours when the days seem to stretch out filled with emptiness.

Of course, how you decide to fill your retirement time is up to you, but initially you may need to make a shift in your mindset about what you could do now that you no longer fill your day with work.

If you are someone who has spent most of your life doing things for others, then deciding what you would really like for yourself might be a challenge for you. However, if you love caring for others but your day seems empty without work, then consider contacting some volunteer agencies, or look in your local paper for indications of volunteers needed in your area. There are usually opportunities for volunteers who want to care for others less able than themselves. These people might be disabled or recovering from an illness and need someone to do some odd jobs for them or just call in for a chat regularly.

You might like to help clear some beaches or build a wall or two and open your eyes to the various opportunities available.

Once you take a bit of time to get used to the idea of not going to work, you might instead want to pursue a learning opportunity to get to grips with a subject you've always been interested in yet never had the time to learn about.

Perhaps you've always wanted to travel to far off places and the first step to doing this might be to learn some conversational phrases in the language of that country.

So don't despair and think you'll be bored when you retire. There is a wealth of things to do or get involved in. Some may involve you spending some of your pension whereas others might be employment so you can increase your income.

Without work routines when you retire, you have days stretching ahead of you and opportunities to do many things you've been dreaming about for years.

FINALLY

Thank-you so much for supporting my work by reading this book.

If you enjoyed it, please let me know by leaving a brief review on the website from which you bought it

It only takes about 30 seconds and is incredibly useful for me as an independent author, and it helps other readers find my books.

Thanks for taking the time to do this. I really, really appreciate it.

Don't miss out!

Visit the website below and you can sign up to receive emails whenever Susan Kersley publishes a new book. There's no charge and no obligation.

https://books2read.com/r/B-A-EFNC-CMDQB

BOOKS 2 READ

Connecting independent readers to independent writers.

Did you love *Retirement: Back to Basics*? Then you should read *Get Ready for Retirement*[1] by Susan Kersley!

Are you apprehensive about having a life after work? Do you wonder how you'll manage without the routine of work? This book will enable you to get ready forretirement.

This book provides you with simple strategies in an easy-to-read format and a step-by-step approach so you can enjoy life after work and make the changes you want to make.

Susan Kersley is a retired Medical Practitioner who became a Life Coach and Writer.

She is the author of personal development books for doctors including 'Prescription for Change for doctors who want a life', 'ABC

---

1. https://books2read.com/u/bPEXl3

2. https://books2read.com/u/bPEXl3

of Change for Doctors,' and 'Life After Medicine.She has also published novels: 'Pills and Pillboxes' and 'Connection Deception.'

Read more at https://susankersley.co.uk.

Also by Susan Kersley

A Novel
Pills and Pillboxes
Connection Deception

Books about Weight Management
Change Your Mind, Change Your Weight
Mind Over Weight
Weight Loss Success

Books for Doctors
ABC of Change for Doctors
Simple Ways to Meet the Challenges of Working as a Doctor
Critical Mistakes Nearly Every Doctor Makes
Life After Medicine
More than 80 ways for a Busy Doctor to have more time
Prescription for Time
Prescription for Change
Work-Life Balance for Doctors
Strategies for Doctors to Connect and Change
Lifestyle Coaching for Doctors

About the Author

Susan Kersley has written personal development and self-help books for doctors and others, and books about retirement and novels.

She was a doctor for thirty years and then left Medicine to be a Life Coach..

Now retired, she is updating her books and writing more. Please visit her website https://susankersley.co.uk

If you enjoyed this book, **please take a moment to leave a review.** Reviews are so important for independent authors.

Read more at https://susankersley.co.uk.